Michael's Mommy Has Breast Cancer

by

Lisa Torrey

Illustrations by Barbara W. Watler

Hibiscus Press

With love to my husband, Kevin, who has always supported my endeavors; to our children, Casey and Sydney, our bright, beautiful gifts from God; and to my parents, William and Dorothy Doyle, for always believing in me.

Warning/Disclaimer

While a serious effort was made to assure that the information provided in this fictional effort is accurate, it is relayed by a layperson and must not be used as a substitute for professional advice, treatment or counseling.

Text and Illustrations Copyright © 1999 by Lisa Torrey.
Published in 1999 by Hibiscus Press
1350 Mhan Drive, Suite E4-158, Tallahassee, FL 32308
(850)216-3262   Fax: (850)656-9703

Printed in the United States of America.   Price $10.95
First Printing, August 1999
Second Printing, December 1999

Publisher's Cataloging-in-Publication
Torrey, Lisa.
Michael's Mommy has breast cancer / by Lisa Torrey. - 1st ed.
p. Cm.
ISBN 0-9647763-6-7
SUMMARY: Michael's family survives a difficult year, as his mother undergoes surgery, radiation treatments, and chemotherapy for breast cancer.
1. Children of cancer patients—Juvenile fiction. 2. Breast—Cancer—Juvenile fiction.
3. Cancer—Patients—Family relationships—Juvenile fiction.
4. Mother and child—Juvenile fiction.   I. Title.
PZ7.T64585Mi 1998   [E]
                                    QBI98-1029
Library of Congress Catalog Card Number: 98-73169

A Message For Adult Readers

Thanks to recent strides in awareness and early detection, many lives of women afflicted with breast cancer in their parenting years are being saved. However, early detection also results in more vulnerable, younger children experiencing the profound impact that the threat of breast cancer has on a family. *Michael's Mommy Has Breast Cancer* addresses the most frequent and universal problems of young children as they have been noted by the American Cancer Society (*Helping Children Understand: A Guide For A Parent With Cancer*) — guilt, anger, fear, and a sad feeling of loss. Families with young children can and do survive the tremendous impact of breast cancer, often feeling closer and stronger than before. Support groups and counseling address the universal problems families experience and assist them in successfully making their way through such trying times.

To locate and contact the support groups available in your area call the American Cancer Society at 1-800-ACS-2345. Hospitals and research centers have also become an excellent resource for family support during severe health crises with child-of-patient support groups now often available. In addition, private and nonprofit counseling centers are becoming more sensitive to these family needs.

Hibiscus Press

Acknowledgments

The support and guidance of Grace Geller, Principal of The Vista School, Coral Springs; Sheryle Baker, M.A., Executive Director of the Life Center, Tampa; and Norma Blackman, M.S., L.M.H.C., of the Family Center in Coral Springs, were greatly appreciated.

A special thanks to surgeon-oncologist Dr. Charles E. Cox, Professor of Surgery at the University of South Florida College of Medicine and Comprehensive Breast Cancer Program Leader at USF's H. Lee Moffitt Cancer Center and Research Institute, for taking time from his extremely busy schedule to provide front-line feedback and the foreword's important message.

My sincere gratitude to the many people who supported and encouraged this effort, including: Sheryl Barton; Rita Mercier Loiselle; Mary Ann Murphy; and my dearest friends, Patty Reynolds, Patti Butler, and Denise Toomy.

I want to express my sincere appreciation to Dorothy Doyle, my editor at Hibiscus Press and my mom, for her invaluable support and expert assistance. Her diagnosis of breast cancer in 1992 started me on this venture.

Last, and most important, I want to thank the families whose real-life stories made this book possible. Their trust and gracious sharing of what our lives become when children and families must cope with mother's breast cancer diagnosis and treatment formed the foundation for Michael's story and truly inspired me.

Michael's Mommy Has Breast Cancer

Foreword

This is a compelling, sensitive book which addresses a significant problem. Few books and little information exist that deal with childhood acceptance of a breast cancer diagnosis. The author empathetically, and in a sensitive way, demonstrates some of the child's concerns and how the family dynamics of interaction over such a delicate issue can be addressed.

This book can serve as a catalyst for continued interaction with children facing this problem. Their fears and concerns as they relate to their mother's illness need to be brought out and discussed. A children's book with this motive is an imperative as younger and younger women are being diagnosed with breast cancer. I congratulate the author and extend the invitation to the reader to be moved by a touching and sensitive approach to a terrifying situation to parent and child alike.

Charles E. Cox, M.D., F.A.C.S.
Professor of Surgery, University of
South Florida College of Medicine -
Program Leader, Comprehensive Breast
Cancer Program, H. Lee Moffitt Cancer
Center and Research Institute at the
University of South Florida

With each step closer to home, Michael knew even more what kind of birthday party he wanted. *When my birthday comes, I want a pizza party just like the one I went to today. I'm going to tell Mommy as soon as I get home.*

Michael walked into his house and knew right away that something was wrong. His news would have to wait. Mom was sitting in the living room waiting for him to return. Her eyes looked red, as if she had been crying.

"Michael, I need to talk to you. Please sit down," she asked.

Michael sat next to his mom, putting his hand on her knee to comfort her. He knew something was very wrong. He was scared.

"Michael, Mommy is sick. I have a lump in my breast. The doctor did a test that showed the lump is cancer," she explained.

"What's cancer?" he questioned.

"Cancer is a sickness that makes a body grow dangerous lumps. To get better, I have to have the lump taken out. I must also have radiation and strong medicine treatments. They will make me tired and sick, but I should be all better when I am done," Mommy explained.

Should be better? "What do you mean *should be better*?" Michael asked anxiously, tears filling his eyes.

"Most women get better, Michael, but some do not. But, Michael, Mommy should get better because the lump is very little," she answered, putting her arm around his shoulder.

Michael's heart sank with sadness. He looked down at the floor and suddenly felt the way he did that awful day last summer when he broke Grandma's favorite crystal vase.

"Michael, there is nothing Mommy, Daddy, or you did that made me sick," she assured him.

Michael looked into his mom's face, wet with tears. He put his arms around her neck. They cried together.

"When will the doctor take it out?" he asked.

"Next week. The radiation starts two weeks later. A machine will put invisible heat inside the dangerous cells and kill them," she explained.

"Will it hurt you?" Michael asked.

"No, radiation doesn't hurt. I will go for six weeks. Then I will have a few months of chemotherapy," she added.

Michael wondered, "What's chemotherapy?"

"The doctor will put very strong medicines in my blood to kill the cancer. They will make me very sick," his mom replied.

"Michael, Mommy is afraid and sad that this has happened to me, but I believe I will be okay," she reminded him with a hug.

A few days later Michael's grandma arrived. He was happy to see her, but sad and scared about Mommy going to the hospital. When it was time for her to leave, Michael wrapped his arms around her and held her real tight.

"I love you, Mommy. Please come home soon," he begged and started to cry.

"Don't worry, Michael, I'll be fine. I will be home tomorrow." She smiled and left with his dad.

      That day at school, Michael couldn't concentrate on his work. Everyone made him angry. After school, he moped around the house. He watched a lot of television, but mostly, he and Grandma waited for the phone to ring.

It rang!

"Is Mommy okay, Grandma?" he asked anxiously. Grandma handed him the phone.

"Mom is doing just fine, Michael," said his dad, happily. "I'll be home in a little while, Son."

Good! That means Mom will be home tomorrow, Michael thought.

The next morning, just as he finished breakfast, his mom came walking through the door.

"Mommy, you're home!" he shouted.

Michael was very relieved that his mom was home, but he was worried. She was so tired and had to rest. Dad said it would be a day or two before Mom felt good again.

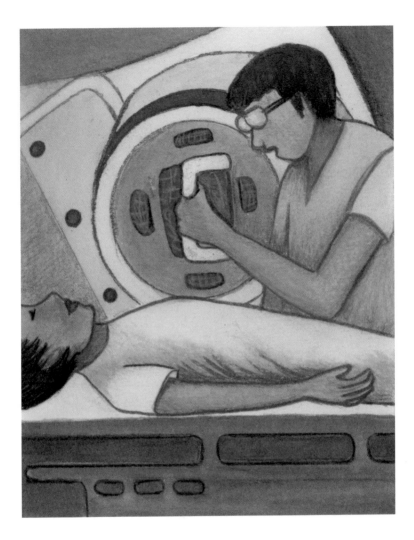

A few weeks later, Mom started her radiation treatments. By the third week she looked tired again and took lots of naps. When Mommy felt okay, she took Michael for ice cream or read him a story.

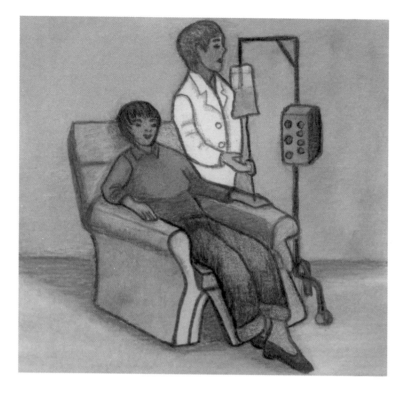

Just before Halloween, Michael's mommy started chemotherapy. The strong medicines made her very sick. All she did was lie down on her bed or on the couch. She didn't want to eat. Michael didn't know what to do. He was frightened and sad. He cried a lot. One day Dad saw him crying. He suggested Michael might feel better inside if he got some juice for Mom. That helped a little, but Michael was still so scared.

That night after dinner, Dad called a family meeting. Mom would not be able to do things around the house as she did before, he explained. They would have to work together to take care of Mom and the household. Dad and Grandma would help Michael with his homework, make his lunches, and read his bedtime stories. Michael would have to help them and take care of their dog, Fred.

Michael was very angry. "Why can't we do things the way we used to?" he demanded, slamming his toy car on the floor.

Dad reminded him, "It's important for us to work together while Mommy is sick, Michael. Mommy needs our help."

"I know," Michael replied sadly.

One day Mommy was sitting on her bed, brushing her hair while Michael was in his room playing. Suddenly, his mother cried out. His father ran down the hall. Michael ran out of his room. His heart was pounding. Mommy was crying. She had a big patch of hair hanging from her hairbrush. Dad told her it would be all right. Her hair would grow back.

Michael quietly slipped back to his room and closed the door. Dad did tell him the strong medicines would make Mommy's hair come out. *What if her hair didn't grow back? What if Mommy didn't get better? What would happen to me and Dad?* he wondered, terribly afraid. His throat hurt. He started to cry.

There was a knock on his door. "Can I come in?" Dad asked.

Michael tried but couldn't talk.

"What's up, Kiddo?" Dad asked, opening the door.

Michael was crying too hard to answer. Then he sobbed, "What will happen to us if Mommy doesn't get better?"

"First, Michael, Mom has a very good chance of getting better. But if she didn't get better, I would take care of you. We would cry and be very sad. We would miss Mommy very much, but we would be okay," Dad assured him with a big hug. Then Dad held him close. Dad wiped the tears from Michael's eyes and his own.

After that day, Dad and Grandma did a lot around the house. They also read him stories and made Michael's lunches. Dad said he felt good knowing he could take care of things for Mom while she was sick. He suggested Michael find more chores to do. Maybe helping more would make him feel better too.

Michael picked up things around the house the next morning. He made sure Fred's dish had plenty of water and food. He brought his mother a glass of juice.

"Thank you, Michael. I really appreciate your help," Mommy said with a smile.

"You're welcome," Michael responded, feeling proud and happy.

"Come sit and talk with me, Son," Mommy said, patting the chair next to her.

It was a special morning, but Michael still just wished that things could be the way they used to.

Michael was often grumpy at school. One day he got into a fight in the lunchroom. The teacher sent his father a note. Dad read the note and was very angry. Michael could not go out to play for two whole days. Nothing was going right. *Mom is always too tired and too sick to do any of our favorite things. Some days I feel so mad! I don't want to help! I want things to be the way they used to be*, Michael pouted.

Finally, Mommy announced one day that her treatments were finished. But she still got tired easily, and they still could not do their favorite things. Dad said it would take time for her strength to come back. Before long, Mommy started reading Michael's bedtime stories. A few weeks later, they went for ice cream.

"Mommy, will I be able to have a big birthday party this year?" Michael asked.

"I'm not sure we will be able to have a big party, Michael, but we'll see," she replied.

One day a couple of months later, Michael's mommy went to the doctor again to see if all the cancer was gone. The doctor tested and checked her over and over again to be sure. Michael felt so alone. He hoped his mom would be okay.

Michael ran home after school just as fast as his legs would go. Mom and Dad were waiting for him in the kitchen. They had great big smiles on their faces.

Mommy walked over and gave him the biggest hug ever. "The doctor says he found no cancer inside me," she said with a playful tickle.

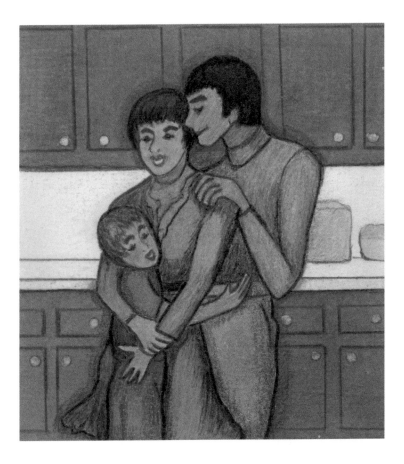

Michael hugged her and didn't want to let go.
He felt so happy inside, he thought he would burst.

"The doctor says I had an excellent recovery,
and, though no one can say for sure, he thinks the
cancer probably will not come back," Mom said with
a squeeze.

It was the happiest day ever. Even better than
birthdays! In a few weeks, it would be Michael's
birthday.

"Mommy, can I have a pizza birthday party this
year?" asked Michael with excitement.

"You bet, Michael. It will be the best pizza
birthday party ever!" she exclaimed.

Not only did Michael have a pizza birthday party, he got the birthday gift he wanted most — he had his Mommy back!

LISA TORREY lives in Coral Springs, Florida, with her husband and their two children. Lisa attended the University of South Florida and Tift College for women in Georgia. She became interested in helping children adjust to their mother's fight against breast cancer in 1992 when her mother - her young son Casey's "nana" - was diagnosed with breast cancer.

BARBARA W. WATLER is an internationally successful artist and illustrator. Her creations appear in a range of media, from watercolor illustrations to contemporary, 3-D thread painting. Barbara lives in Hollywood, Florida. She is a breast cancer survivor who lost her mother to the illness.

To Make Arrangements For Lisa Torrey To Speak To Your Group: Contact Hibiscus Press at 1-800-468-4004.

To Order:

Michael's Mommy Has Breast Cancer

<u>Telephone Orders</u>: Call 1-800-468-4004

<u>Internet Orders</u>: http://www.amazon.com or
http://www.barnesandnoble.com

<u>Mail Orders</u>: Hibiscus Press, 1350 Mahan Drive, Suite
E4-158, Tallahassee, FL 32308. Send check or money order
in the amount of $10.95 + 1.00 shipping ($11.95); FL
residents add $.82 (7.5%) Sales Tax (Total: $12.77).

<u>Reseller/Quantity Purchases</u>: Telephone (850)216-3262 or
1-800-468-4004 or fax (850)656-9703 or write to: Hibiscus
Press, 1350 Mahan Drive, Suite E4-158, Tallahassee, FL

Special! Save Over 20%

Order *Michael's Mommy Has Breast Cancer* ($10.95) along
with its widely acclaimed adult companion book, *Dancing
On The Edge*, an uplifting, inspiring breast cancer story
and resource guide by Dorothy Palmieri Doyle ($14.95), and
save. Call 1-800-468-4004.

A $25.90 value for $19.95